Anonymous

A Letter to a Member of Parliament, Shewing the Necessity of Regulating the Press

Cheifly from the necessity of publick establishments in religion, from the rights and immunities of a National Church, and the trust reposed in the Christian magistra

Anonymous

A Letter to a Member of Parliament, Shewing the Necessity of Regulating the Press

Cheifly from the necessity of publick establishments in religion, from the rights and immunities of a National Church, and the trust reposed in the Christian magistra

ISBN/EAN: 9783337377090

Printed in Europe, USA, Canada, Australia, Japan

Cover: Foto ©Lupo / pixelio.de

More available books at **www.hansebooks.com**

A LETTER

TO A

Member of Parliament,

Shewing the Necessity of

Regulating the PRESS:

CHIEFLY
From the Necessity of Publick Establishments in RELIGION.

From the Rights and Immunities of a National ~~Church.~~

And the Trust reposed in the Christian Magistrate to Protect and Defend them.

WITH
A Particular ANSWER *to the* OBJECTIONS *that of late have been Advanced against it.*

OXFORD:
Printed for *George West*, and *Henry Clements*.
M. DC. XCIX.

The CONTENTS.

AN *Enquiry into the Duty of the* Magiftrate *in matters of Religion:* Sect. 1. *Confidered, firft, under a ftate of* Nature, Ib. *Secondly, under a ftate of* Revelation: Sect. 2.

An Objection anfwered: Sect. 3.

An Enquiry when there are two or more Sects of Religion in any Government, why the Magiftrate is under an obligation of protecting, or rather advancing the one more than the other: Sect. 4, *and* 5.

The Rights and Authority of a National Church *confidered and ftated:* Sect. 5.

The Reftraint *of the* Prefs *demonftrated, not only as it is a neceffary provifion to advance the Interefts of* Religion, *but to preferve and maintain the Ends and Defigns of it, as profeffed in a National Church:* Sect. 6.

The Neceffity of Publick Eftablifhments in Religion, and the pernicious Influences which the Liberty of the Prefs *has upon them, as introductory of* Scepticifm, Herefie *and* Infidelity: Sect. 7, 8, *and* 9.

The Argument reprefented in feveral Inftances from fome late Prints: Sect. 8, 9. *Objections anfwered.*

As

The Contents.

As first, That the Attempts and Mischiefs of the Press, *may as effectually be obviated by particular Laws, and that a* Restraint of the Press *from the Experience of former times has not prevented 'em:* Sect. 10.

Secondly, That a Restraint *of the* Press *is a giving up of the Consciences and Judgments of Mankind to a Party, and a Condemning them to an Implicit Faith, and is a direct Method to involve the World in Ignorance and Error:* Sect. 11.

The Church of England *denies no Gospel means of Information:* Sect. 12.

Thirdly, That every one, not only of Natural Right, but in point of Charity, may, and ought to publish whatever appears to be Truth; and consequently the Restraint *of the* Press, *which abridges this Right, must be unlawful, and unjust:* Sect. 13.

The Natural Rights of Private Persons in the Case before us, stated: Sect. 14.

The Duty of Informing others stated: Ib.

Fourthly, That the Restraint *of the* Press, *is an Invasion of the Liberty, and Property of an* Englishman: Sect. 15.

The Conclusion, in an Address to the Honourable Member: Sect. 16.

A

A LETTER

TO A

Member of Parliament;

SHEWING

The Necessity of Regulating the PRESS: With a Particular ANSWER to the OBJECTIONS that of late have been advanced against it.

SIR,

YOU have been pleas'd to sollicite my Opinion in a Matter of Importance, by way of Request, when You might *have* justly *lay'd Your* Commands; and I now present it with all imaginable *Deference* and *Humility.* You have led me into a large Field of *Argument,* and propos'd several *weighty Enquiries;* but since they are advanced with regard to a

Gene-

General Design, viz. The *Liberty of the* PRESS; I shall not bind my self up to that Order they are propos'd in, but shall speak to them, as they will best comport with the Scheme I have projected, to evince the *Expediency of Restraining the Press*.

In order to this Design, I shall reduce them to three or four General Enquiries.

As first, *How far the Duty of the Civil Governing Powers extends in Matters of Religion?*

Secondly, *When there are two or more Sects of Religion in any Government, why the Magistrate is under an Obligation of protecting, or rather advancing the one, more than the other:* And on this Head I shall consider the Rights and Authority of a National Church.

Thirdly, *Whether the Restraint of the Press is not a necessary provision, not only to advance the Interests of the true Religion, but to preserve and maintain the Ends and Designs of it, as profess'd in a National Church?*

SECT.

SECT. I. I begin with an *Enquiry into the Duty of the Civil Governing Powers in Matters of Religion.*

And, First, It will be received as an indisputable *Article*, or *Proposition*, That every *Governing Power* (of *Duty* as well as *Right*) is so far to inspect the Affair of *Religion*, that nothing be advanced, that manifestly incommodes the Rights or Interests of the *Civil Polity*: But whether any Government, is under a further Concern or Obligation, seems to be the Case under debate. Now it will best be adjusted by considering the *Nature* and *Design* of Civil Government; first under a state of *Nature*, and secondly under a state of *Revelation*.

That Government in general is an *Ordinance of* GOD, *by Divine Institution*, as well as *Allowance*, and consequently that there are certain *Ends* and *Designs* peculiar to it, established in the same Authority, are Truths that will be easily subscribed to. But then if Government rests on a *Divine Original*, and there are certain Divine Ends and Purposes appropriate to it; it cannot well be imagin'd that the *Civil*

Welfare and Conduct of Mankind, is the sole and entire Province of the *Civil Magistrate*. If *Religion* is the most important Concern of Mankind; and if there's *Fealty*, *Worship*, and *Obedience*, due from a *Creature* towards a Sovereign *Creator*, even under the most simple state of Nature; why should not that Great GOD, which constitutes the Civil Magistrates *Superintendants* over the Secular affairs of Mankind, be as zealous to make them *Guardians* of those things that are placed more near him, and them too, his *Honour* and *Glory*? And therefore I'm perswaded it's neither Boldness nor Arrogance to pronounce, That the Civil *Governing Power*, or *Magistrate*, was originally constituted for the Conduct of Mankind, in all the Instances of *Human Happiness;* and consequently in a *Religious* as well as *Civil* Capacity. Indeed the inseparable Dependance and Affinity, between *Civil Happiness* and *Religion*, (were other Arguments wanting) is alone sufficient to evince it: But were the Experience of Mankind, and the universal Practice of all Civiliz'd Governments, summoned in to decide the Con-

Controversy, they must place it above Dispute, or Cavil. If we respect the earliests Accounts of Governments, and particularly those delivered in Sacred Story, we find the Characters of *Prince* and *Priest*, residing in the same Person.

Before GOD had instituted a *positive Oeconomy* of Religion, and a peculiar Order of *Priesthood*, it was part of the *Patriarchal* province, not only to instruct their People to *call upon the Name of the Lord*, but to wait on the very *Altar*; and perform the Priestly Function of *Sacrifices*. As *it's highly probable from the History of the Creation*, the first Governments of the World, had their Rise and Foundation in Fathers of Families; so we are undoubtedly instructed that they obtained the Character of *Patres patriæ*, by executing all the Offices of a *Parent*, as well as *King*. *Abraham* had no doubt his Duty represented as a *Prince*, as well as *Master* of a *Family*, under the Compliment of a Divine Confidence: for *I know him that he will command his Children, and his houshold after him, and they shall keep the way of the Lord, to do justice and judgment,* Gen.

Gen. 18. 19. And truly since both *Prince* and *Parent*, have the Impress of *Divine Authority* upon 'em; and there is such a strict Affinity and Correspondence between 'em, from the original frame of things; if the Character of a *Parent* extends to a *Religious* as well as *Civil* Capacity, it cannot well be disputed, but that of a *Prince* carries the same extent and latitude. And therefore it may safely be concluded, that it was a point of Duty in the *Magistrate*, antecedent to any *positive Oeconomy* of *Religion*, to promote the Interests, if not execute the Spiritual Functions of *Religion*, as well as advance the Welfare of the State: And very probably it was a Divine Institution, as ancient and primitive as Government it self.

And certainly the Model of all Heathen Governments confirms the Notion. It's well known the *Egyptian Monarchs* (Famous in the earliest Records) bare the Character of *Priest*, as well as *King*. The *Chinese* to this Day, look upon the Priesthood to bear so near a Relation to that of the Empire, that the most Solemn Mysteries of Religion, are still a Prerogative pecu-

peculiar to the *Sovereign*. Religion in the Eastern and Western parts of *Europe*, was always so much the Business of Government, that if the publick Acts and Offices of Religion were not immediately perform'd by the *Magistrate*, they were constantly directed, and enforc'd by him. If the publick Defence of a Countrey, where its Territories were enlarged and extended, diverted him from attending the *Altar*, it was his special Care to constitute a *Priesthood*, and regulate the Affairs of *Religion*, by publick Laws and Sanctions: these are such known and allow'd Truths, and so well attested, in the Learning of the *Greeks* and *Latins*, that I shall not now appeal to *Authors*; and they are all convincing Evidences, that one End of Government, in the original Frame and Model of it, was to *inspect* the Conduct of Mankind in the *Affairs* of *Religion*. Thus far not only the *Duty*, but *Prerogative* of the *Magistrate* discovers it self in a State of Nature, antecedent to Revelation.

SECT.

SECT. II. It remains that we consider it under a positive Oeconomy of Religion.

And, first, under that of the *Jews*. Now tho' GOD thought fit upon the first positive Establishment of Religion, to institute an Order of Men, and separate them from the rest of the People, to attend at his *Altar*, to *offer for themselves, and the sins of others*; yet it's manifest he did not exempt the Civil *Magistrate* from inspecting the Affairs of *Religion*. No, it was his special Duty, to protect and defend the *True Religion*; to punish and suppress *Idolatry, Seducers*, and *False Prophets*, and to make such wholesom provisions, as served the cause of Religion, in the enforcement of its *Publick Acts* and *Offices*, and in the Advancement of its *Ends* and *Designs*. The Sacred Writings have delivered so many Instances, and Rules of this Nature, that it is wholly needless to enlarge in an express Citation. It's well known he often directed the Building of places of *Religious Worship*, enjoyn'd *Fasts*; and in a word, interpos'd in most of the Circumstantials of *Religion*. Now it's certain

certain these were not bare *Arbitrary Offices*, and the product of a *Voluntary Zeal*; but they were either the immediate Instruction of *Heaven*, or the effects of some *General Precepts*; and consequently were intended as standing Instances of *Duty*. If we examine the œconomy of the *Gospel*, we must conclude, That as we have not the least hint that any ways abridges the *Rights* and *Authority* of the Civil *Magistrate*, further than they were exercised under the *Law*, so we do not find the least Exemption from any Moral point of *Duty* in the Affairs of *Religion*, to which they were antecedently bound. Now it cannot be deny'd, but that the Nature and State of the *Christian Church* is frequently describ'd in the Writings of the *Prophets:* And among those various Descriptions, the Character of *Christian Kings* and *Princes*, recorded by the Prophet *Isaiah*, is as glorious as it is remarkable: *And Kings shall be thy nursing Fathers, and their Queens thy nursing Mothers*————*for they shall not be ashamed that wait for me, Isa.* 44. *v.* 23. This Passage is unanimously interpreted of the *Christian Magistrate;* and certainly we are not to receive it as a Prediction of a *Contingent Blessing,* or *Matter of Fact,* but agreeable to the *Prophetick* Style (which often exhibits Duties, under simple Predictions) as carrying the Force of a *Precept* in it. Thus we see the *Magistrate* is not only *Pater Patriæ,* but *Pater Ecclesiæ.* This is his *Character,* and his *Duty:* and certainly, if he answers the Designs of it, he must not only *cherish,* but *protect,* and *defend* the Church of *Christ;* and in a word, liberally minister to it, whatever is necessary for its *Support* and *Preservation.* Upon the whole then, we may justly conclude, That tho' God, under the *Jewish,* as well as *Gospel* œconomy, was pleased to select a peculiar Order of Men, to wait on his Altar, and more immediately prosecute all the Designs of Religion; yet the Civil Magistrate still rightfully ministers to the same Designs in all Cases, where God has not interposed by some *Positive Rule,* or *Precept;* so that he's still the *Supreme Guardian* and *Protector,* in the *œconomy* of *Religion,* as well as *Civil Polity.* He's *Custos utriusque*

usque Tabulæ; that is, he's not only entrusted to enforce the Observance of all *Social Vertues,* upon which the *Peace* and *Interest* of Government moves, as upon its *Axis;* but a *True* and *Orthodox Faith,* and a *pure Worship,* and the *Honour* and *Glory* of that *Great* God, that has made him his *Vicegerent* and *Representative;* and by whose *Protection* and *Blessing* he's enabled to answer the *Designs* of his *Character.*

From hence the Dis-ingenuity, or rather Impiety of some late designing Positions, abundantly discover themselves; viz. *That the care of* Religion *is no real Branch of the* Magistrate's *Office; that he's no further concerned for it, than as it immediately conduces to the Civil Weal and Interest of every particular Constitution or Government; and in a word, That for the advance of a National Trade or Wealth, he may treat all Sects of* Religion *with equal privileges and respect.* But certainly the care of Religion can now no longer be disputed, to be an *Indispensible Duty* in the Magistrate; since it appears not only that every Positive Oeconomy of Religion, has

ex-

expresly taught it; but the very *Nature, Designs,* and *Reasons* of the *Character,* dictate it.

But then, if this be admitted, we must grant that there is a *True* and a *False Religion,* and an *Orthodox* and *Heterodox Faith;* that the true Religion is established on certain Laws, and Immunities, which in the ordinary course of Providence, are necessary to the Preservation of it; and consequently we must conclude, That it's an Indispensible Duty in the Magistrate, to have recourse to the most proper Methods for enquiring into the *Reasons* and *Grounds* of *Religion;* and for distinguishing the *True Religion* from the *False,* and an *Orthodox* from an *Heterodox Faith;* whether by applying to the proper *Ministers* of *Religion, separately,* or in *Council.* And upon a fair and impartial Enquiry, that which appears to be True and Orthodox, is to be *cherished, defended,* and *promoted,* against all Attempts and Invasions of the *Heterodox* and *Unbeliever;* even tho' some present Temporal Interest seem to clash and interfere with it. These were the *Unalterable Laws* and *Principles*
of

of the firſt and *moſt pious Chriſtian Empe-rors*, upon which they enlarged the *Territories* of the Chriſtian Church.

Sect. III. But to this 'tis *popularly* reply'd, That if Kings and Princes once thought themſelves obliged to eſpouſe the Care of Religion, as a poſitive Duty (conſidering the Errors and Superſtitions of Mankind) it would prove the moſt effectual Method, not only to obſtruct the growth of the True Religion, but endanger the Extirpation of it. But in anſwer to this, it's to be conſidered, That the Propagation of Religion does not direct to Acts of force and violence, much leſs the Protection of it; except where the Rights and Immunities of the Eſtabliſhed Religion are apparently invaded. Beſides it's concluded the Magiſtrate is not to proceed *blindly*, but apply himſelf to the True *Means* of *Information*; and if he miſcarries, tho' he may one day anſwer for any *Siniſter Motives*, that carried him into a wrong Determination; yet God will find Methods to ſupport his own Deſigns, and conſequently advance the Intereſts of
the

the True Religion, by Secret and Invisible Springs, tho' his Ordinary and Standing Provisions afford the most unlikely Prospect. Sometimes Persecution it self is the most prolifick Soil for the True Religion to shoot forth and flourish in: *Christianity* had not only its first Foundation in it, but we are assured received Great Increases from it. So *Tertullian* in his *Apologetic* boasts, *Nec quicquam tamen*, says he, *proficit exquisitior quæque crudelitas vestra*, ILLECEBRA EST MAGIS SECTÆ. *Plures efficimur quoties metimur a vobis.* SEMEN EST SANGUIS CHRISTIANORUM. *Tertull. Apolog.* pag. 45.

But in a word, if the Care of Religion is a standing Duty, in the Magistrate; (as has been abundantly evinced) and if there be such a thing as a True Religion, and sufficient Means (if duly attended to) to distinguish it from the False; the Undoubted *Rule* is, That the *Duty* is to be *pursued*, and the Consequences left to the Providential *Care* of the Blessed *Author* of it; who has the Hearts of *Kings*, and the Sovereign Disposal of *Grace*, and will

will in the Course of Affairs undoubtedly ascertain the *Usefulness* of his own Means, and the *Ends* of *Religion* for which they were designed. And as for that Magistrate, who upon a Principle of Zeal for the Honour of his *Maker*, shall thus carry on the Designs of the True Religion, he'll no doubt one Day be made partaker of a Reward, that will every way answer *that labour of love, which he has shewed towards his Name;* he'll one Day infallibly find a Remembrance, sutable to the Supplications of that Excellent Governour *Nehemiah, Remember me, O my* GOD, *concerning this, and wipe not out my good deeds that I have done for the House of my* GOD, *and for the offices thereof, Neh.* 13. v. 14.

SECT. IV. I proceed to the second Enquiry, *viz. When there are two, or more Sects of Religion under any Government, why the Magistrate is under an Obligation of protecting, or rather advancing the one, more than the other?*

And *First*, I shall consider this Argument, with regard to the *Oeconomy* of the *Christian Church*. And in order to this
it

it will be requisite to enquire into the Rights, and Authority of a *National Church*.

And, *First*, its indisputably evident the *Christian Church* is one *Society*, or *Body* of Men united to Christ, and *each other* in certain *External*, as well as *Internal* and *Spiritual* Bonds of Union. It's truly a *Seamless Garment*; nay, it bears the Exact Portraicture of a *Natural* Body, *whereof* Christ *is the Head, from whom the whole Body fitly joyn d together, and compacted by that which every joynt supplieth, according to the effectual working in the measure of every part, maketh increase of the Body*, Eph. 4. 16. In a word, it carries the Symmetry and Proportion of a *Building, fitly framed together, growing into an holy Temple in the* Lord, *Eph* 2. 21. The first Division of this Spiritual Body, arises from the *Necessity of Divine Worship*; viz. into particular Congregations. Other Distributions arise from the *Necessity* of *Government*, which is warranted and established, by the express *Canon* of Scripture. Thus, *Obey them that have the rule over you, and submit your selves, for they watch for*

for your Souls, Heb. 13. 17. And St. *Paul's* Inſtructions to *Titus* are, *For this cauſe I left thee in* Crete, *that thou ſhouldeſt ſet in order the things that are wanting*, Ch. 1. ver. 5. And, *Theſe things ſpeak and exhort, and rebuke with all Authority*, Ch. 2o. We may add to this, the *Power* of *Binding* and *Looſing*, and *Excommunication* it ſelf, being expreſly committed to the *Eccleſiaſtical Powers*; and evidently demonſtrating the *Neceſſity*, as well as *Divine Authority* of Eccleſiaſtical Government.

But to return: Whatever Diſtributions were made, either from a Neceſſity of Worſhip, or Government, every Branch or Part, is indiſpenſibly bound to maintain this Myſtical Union; by a Communion in the Eſſentials of *Faith, Government*, and *Diſcipline*: for otherwiſe it's impoſſible the *Chriſtian Church* ſhould anſwer the Character of a *Natural Body fitly joyned together, and compacted by that which every joynt ſupplieth, even to the making increaſe of the Body*.

As for the Government of the Church, we are aſſured, partly from *Scripture*, and partly from the *earlieſt Antiquity*, That the

the Order of *Bishops* and *Metropolitans*, rests on *Apostolical Institution*. Both *Timothy* and *Titus*, in the judgement of the most Learned *Presbyterians*, were Superior to the rest of the *Clergy*, within their *Districts*, at least in *Jurisdiction*, if not *Order*. And tho' *Antiquity* has not expresly fix'd the Origine or Rise of *Metropolitans*, yet it may justly be presum'd to be *Apostolical*.

For *First*, St. *Paul* directs an Epistle to the Metropolitical Church, to be communicated to the whole Province; for such was *Corinth* in the Province of *Achaia*. *To the Church of* GOD, *which is at* Corinth, *with all the Saints that are in all* Achaia. And, pursuant to this, we find the Governments of *Metropolitans* in the first Council of *Nice*, ranked among the Ἀρχαῖα ἔθη, *Ancient Customs, Can.* 6. and in that of *Antioch*, styled Ἀρχαιότερον κρατήσαντα πάτρων ἐκ τ̅ ἡμῶν κανόνα, The *most ancient Canon in force, from the times of our Forefathers*. But that which conduces to the present Argument, is, *That all the Establishments of Church Government, and the Districts of particular Churches, were originally modeled*

deled according to that of the State. The Bishop presided over a City, and the adjacent Villages and Territories; where a Temporal Magistrate was likewise placed. As the *Metropolis* of every Province had its *Proconsul* in the *State*, so it had its *Archbishop*, or *Metropolitan* in the *Church*. And when the Government of *Patriarchs* prevailed, it was formed after the same Model, either in Imitation of the *Vicars*, or *Lieutenants* that presided over a *Diocese*, composed of several Provinces; or at least in Imitation of the *Pretorian Prefects*, that had several *Dioceses* under their Jurisdiction.

Upon the whole then, as we are assured, That the forming a Government in the Church, after the Model of that of the State, was by *Apostolical Institution*; so we may justly conclude, that it was by the special Directions of the *Holy Spirit*. And, no doubt, the great Design was to advance the Interests of *Religion*, by placing every particular *Church* under the *Protection* of the *State*, whenever it should become *Christian*. And certainly, as it was the only true Expedient to enable the Civil

Magiftrate, to execute that Truft, that is lodged in the Character of a *Father*, or *Nurfing Mother*, to the Church of *Chrift*; fo it's a confiderable Argument that the Care and Protection of the True Religion is a ftanding Duty, incumbent on the *Civil Magiftrate*. For to make the Diftricts of particular Churches, terminate with thofe of Civil Governments, was abfolutely neceffary, to make the *Civil Magiftrate* the Supreme Guardian of the True Religion: and, fince 'tis an Ordinance, that may very juftly be refolved into *Apoftolick Inftitution*, it's a manifeft Indication, that the Civil Magiftrate fhould be obliged punctually to anfwer the Character, whenever he became *Chriftian*.

SECT. V. From hence we may gain a true Notion of the Rights and Authority of a *National Church*. And truly, if we duly weigh the Premifes, we muft conclude, That it refts upon nothing lefs than *Divine* and *Apoftolick* Inftitution. For if the *Apoftles* themfelves conftituted particular Churches, with regard to the Diftricts of particular Provinces, and the Government

vernment of the State; and if it be a standing Duty in the Christian Magistrate, to protect and advance the *True Religion*, within his Dominions; we must conclude, That a Church is to be established upon that Model of Government, which was instituted by our Saviour, or his Apostles, in every respective Nation, over which the Magistrate is to preside, as a *Father*, or *Guardian*, and *Protector;* and such a *Church* is what in other terms is called a *National Church;* and a Church thus established, undoubtedly rests on the Authority of *Divine* or *Apostolick* Institution.

I would not be mistaken, as if I intended to deny the being of a *National* or *Provincial Church*, till it has obtain'd a *Civil Establishment;* for it's manifest, the Churches of *Greece*, and of the *Proconsular Asia*, had a being, and a distinct Denomination, before *Christianity* was received in the *Courts* of *Princes*. Indeed when a particular Church enjoys a *Civil Establishment*, it receives, as it were, a new *Authority;* in as much as it becomes a *Civil Right* or *Property:* So that unless its Constitution is *Materially* vitious and sinful, it's a high piece of injustice

justice to destroy or infringe any of its *Established Rights*, or *Immunities*. But yet since the Magistrate is only the *Guardian*, not the *Founder* of a National Church, (its Original Authority resting on certain positive *Laws*, and *Sanctions*, enjoyned by a Power superiour to that of the Magistrate, even that of GOD *Himself*) where-ever a Church in any Province or Nation, professes the True Religion by an Orthodox Faith, and a pure Worship, under *Lawful Church Governours* and *Pastors*, that is the *True National Church*, in opposition to all dissenting *Sects* and *Parties;* tho' it wants the Authority of a *Civil Establishment*.

But to return: From hence we may easily determine the merits of the Question in debate, I mean *When there are two, or more Sects of Religion in any Government, why the Magistrate is under an Obligation of protecting, or rather advancing the one, more than the other?*

For, *First*, it is abundantly demonstrated that the Christian Magistrate, *ex officio*, is constituted a *Guardian, Father*, and *Protector* of the True Religion; and there-

therefore if in any Nation, or Government, the true Religion is profeſſed in an *Orthodox*, and a *pure Worſhip*, under *lawful Church Governours* and *Paſtors*; there the Magiſtrate is indiſpenſibly bound to act as a Guardian and Protector, in oppoſition to all Models, and Platforms that are advanced againſt it. For by this alone he purſues the Great Deſign of the *Apoſtolick Platform*, in the Inſtitution of *National Churches*, as well as anſwers that of his Character; I mean as he's Prophetically ſtyled, a *Father* to the Church of CHRIST.

It's certain one Great Deſign of Chriſtianity, is *Unity*; or to range all the Parts and Members of the Church of CHRIST into an *Holy Building*: and therefore, if the Magiſtrate is conſtituted a Guardian of the True Religion, all his Offices of *Succour* and *Protection* muſt be directed to this End; I mean the maintainance of the Bonds of *Catholick Unity*, throughout his whole Dominions. Without this, the Great Ends, and Propoſals of ſo pure and holy a Religion, cannot be accompliſhed; and therefore whatever Indulgences, or Exemptions the Chriſtian Magiſtrate may right-

rightfully grant to *Erroneous Judgments*, or *Consciences*, acted with simplicity and a pious Disposition; he cannot upon the *Laws and Oeconomy of the Gospel, or any Authority derived to him from thence*, *rightfully* give a *Positive Establishment*, within the Districts of the same Government, to two *Opposite Communions*, or *Altars* of *Worship*; especially when one of them is founded in a revolt, from a *pure* and *Orthodox National Church*. This is the very reverse to a *Protector* and *Defender* of the True Religion. For it implies a power to *pervert* the Great Design of the Christian Religion; *viz.* a *Unity* of *Faith* and *Worship*; by dissolving the Bonds of *Catholick Unity*, and Authorizing the Members of CHRIST's *Mystical Body*, to disband and break into *Schisms* and *Factions*: whereas it's an External Rule, That the *Magistrate* can only challenge a Power to *Edification*, not to *Destruction*. This is so far from being a Prerogative of the Magistrate, that where a National Church is constituted under *Lawful Governours* and *Pastors*, tho' there may be some Defects, or Errors in her *Faith, Discipline,*

scipline, or *Worship;* he's not to *unhinge* and *demolish*, but to endeavour to *correct* and *remove* them, by such *Means* and *Instruments*, as GOD, in his revealed Will, has decreed and appointed: and when this is done, he's not to suffer any opposite *Sects*, or *Factions*, so much as to *break in* upon any of her *Apostolick Rights*, or *Immunities*. For it's manifest, the Duty of a *Guardian*, *Parent* and *Protector*, is to use all prudent Methods to *cultivate* and *improve*, to *advance* the *Interests*, and *enlarge* the *Priviledges* of those under his Care; much more to defend them from *Violence*, or *Incroachment*. To be appointed a *Father*, and a *Protector* of CHRIST's Church, or the True Religion, is not an Empty Name, but carries very momentous Offices and Duties in it: it implies a *Zeal* for the *Honour of* GOD, and the *True Religion;* and consequently it engages the Magistrate to study such wholesom Provisions, as will advance the Ends and Interests of it, to the utmost Boundaries of his Dominions: and those that thus *wait for* CHRIST, *shall not be ashamed, Isai.* 49. *v.* 23.

And now, *Sir*, I hope I have prepared You for the main Argument You proposed, by informing You how the Magistrate is determined, for the Interests of Religion, and particularly those of this *National Church*.

SECT. VI. I shall proceed to consider, *Whether the Restraint of the* PRESS, *is not a Necessary Provision, not only to advance the Interests of the True Religion, but to preserve, and maintain the Ends and Designs of it, as profess'd in a National Church?* And this will appear from the *Necessity* of a publick Establishment in Religion, and the *Pernicious Influences*, which the *Liberty* of the *Press* has upon it.

It's already concluded, that GOD has instituted a Governing Power in the Christian Church; and the accommodating it to the Districts of the State, and the Constituting the Civil Magistrate a *Guardian*, and *Protector* of the Church of CHRIST, is at least a sufficient Warrant of the *Lawfulness* of a publick Establishment, if not an Indication of its *Necessity*.

In-

Indeed since there are Governing Powers in the Church of CHRIST, we must conclude, that GOD foresaw a great many Difficulties and Miscarriages, under the great Revolutions and Emergencies of Human Affairs; which he has Authorized them to *adjust, correct* and *remove:* and this will justly infer the Necessity of publick *Decrees, Articles,* or *Canons,* and that too in Matters of *Faith, Worship,* and *Practice.* It cannot be denied, but *Scripture* it self has established the Authority of such Powers, and Injunctions; and consequently it's an indisputable Argument of their *Necessity:* since GOD never imparts special Powers, or Functions, but he infallibly discerns the Necessity and Usefulness of 'em. Thus we have General Rules directed to particular Churches, in the business of Publick Worship, *That things be prescribed, and done according to the Laws of Decency, Order, and Edification.* And no doubt St. *Paul* points at the same thing, when he reminds *Titus,* why he placed him over the Church of *Crete, That thou shouldst set in order the things that are wanting:* Tit. 1. 5. So that we may justly conclude, there's a Power given to prescribe such Laws and Rules, and make such Publick Declarations, as manifestly tend to the *Edifying the Body of Christ;* or as are requisite to maintain the Catholick Laws of Unity, or the *Unity of the Spirit, in the bond of peace.*

But to descend to particulars. And *first*, as to matters of Faith; Indeed it will be easily granted, That the Holy Scriptures are a compleat *Rule* of *Faith;* and consequently they seem to be a competent Standard, for the Governours of particular Churches, to try the *Faith* of *Christians* by. But yet we are assured that they contain a *Great many things, hard to be understood, which the ignorant and unlearned wrest to their own destruction;* and consequently things of the greatest moment, and importance. Again, we are assured, that *Heresies* will come, that there will arise *False Christs*, and *False Prophets*, and *Men of corrupt Minds*, who have not only *erred*, but are *reprobate concerning the Faith*. In a word, it's impossible but Controversies and Divisions, as well as Offences, will come; this is the case of every

every Tribe, or Colony of *Christians*.

And is there no Judgment to be made in these Circumstances? Are these Persons to be suffered to proceed in their Errors, and *pervert* the *Faith* of others? If this must be so, for what End has the Blessed Author of our Religion placed *Governours* and *Pastors* in his Church, and enforced their Authority by the Discipline of special Censure? They cannot remonstrate against them, without making a Judgment whether the *Doctrine be of* God, or is consonant to the *Canon* of *Faith*. And yet 'tis their Duty to declare the *whole Counsel of* God in these Cases. And certainly, if *Private Pastors* are Authorized to expound the Sence of Scripture, and make a Judgment in these Matters, and expect the Directions of the Holy Spirit, to wait on their pious Labours, and Endeavours; much more may an *Assembly*, or *Council* of *Church-Governours* interpose, state the Sence of Scripture, and deliver a Definitive Sentence in express *Articles* and *Decrees*, and expect the Influences of the same *Spirit* in the whole performance. Certainly, where *two or three*, or more, are for these Ends

Ends *gathered together*, (it may juftly be prefumed) GOD *will be in the midst of 'em.*

Thefe are Proceedings warranted by the Practice of the College of Apoftles, and of all particular Churches, from their Days, to this very Hour: Such Errors, Divifions, and Mifcarriages *concerning* the *Faith* authorized, and gave birth to the *Confeſſions* of *Faith*, in all Particular Churches. They were the only Barriers againſt *Hereſie* and *Error*, and indifpenfibly neceffary, to preferve the *Unity* of the *Faith*, and the *Church* of CHRIST, from Diftraction and Ruine. To affirm that Scripture in thefe Cafes is a fufficient Rule, and reject all Interpofals, or Determinations purfuant to it, is to miftake or perplex the Argument. For tho' Scripture is an adequate Rule of Faith, and Manners; yet GOD has conftituted *Guardians* and *Truſtees*, to affert the Sence of Scripture, and enforce a Faith and Practice, conformable to it: and to deny this, is in effect to difcard the neceffity of any *Viſible Miniſtry*; fince Scripture, with the help of private Reafon, is as much an adequate

quate Rule in this respect, as the other; and consequently there could be no necessity of a standing Ministry. It's true, these *Publick Determinations*, these *Confessions* of *Faith*, are not established upon a *Spirit* of *Infallibility*: but they are not to be rejected, or less *necessary*; because not *Infallible*. GOD has not thought fit to impart a Spirit of Infallibility, in the Exercise of the *Power* of *Excommunication*; yet Scripture establishes it as a *Standing Ordinance* in his Church. A Spirit of Infallibility does not accompany the *Ministerial Function*; and yet GOD has made it absolutely necessary. In a word then, in as much as they are Decisions grounded on *Scripture*, supported by *Reason*, and confirm'd by the joynt *Authority* and *Suffrage* of the *Church* of GOD, in the earliest Ages, and of *Saints, Confessors* and *Martyrs*; they are the most apposite Moral Instruments, under GOD, and the use of *Reason*, to determine the *Judgment*, and satisfie the *Conscience*; or at least to stop the Mouths of *Gainsayers*, as far as concerns the outward *Peace* of the *Church*.

In this Case, they become indispensibly necessary; there must be some External Umpire and Decision, where Matters must at last terminate: that the publick Peace and Unity (things in the judgment of our Blessed Saviour, of the greatest value and importance) may not be sacrificed to the Dissentions, Heats, and Animosities of Corrupt and Restless Spirits.

If such Decrees, or Injunctions are not to be imposed as *Essentials* of *Faith*, or *Terms* of *Communion*; yet they are, in the Language of our Church, to be received as Injunctions *for the avoiding Diversity of Opinions, and for establishing Consent touching True Religion:* Or, in one word, as *Articles* of *Peace;* so that whosoever publickly oppugns 'em, is at least to be censured, as a Breaker of the Peace of the Church.

But further, as to the Duty of *Publick Worship*, it's undeniably evident, the great *Circumstantials* of Worship are no where determined in Scripture, such as the *Time*, *Manner*, and *Place;* and yet these are Moral, and inseparable Circumstances, without which 'tis impossible the Duty

Duty can be performed. And therefore it's absolutely necessary, they should be committed to the Determination of those Powers and Authorities, GOD has constituted in his Church. For tho' this, or that *Particular Determination* be not necessary, till 'tis settled; yet it's absolutely necessary, they should be *determined some way or other*. And this demonstrates the Necessity of Publick Establishments, in the Duties of Publick Assemblies, and Publick Worship.

Again, as to the Case of Discipline, how can that *Decency, Order,* and *Uniformity,* which the Word of GOD so passionately recommends, be maintained without the Establishment of Districts, and the Settlement of Time and Place? how can the Manners of Men be animadverted on, or their Neglects, or Irregularities in the Publick Worship of GOD be censured? what must become of the Publick Duties of *Admonition* and *Reproof,* and *Exclusion* from the *External Means* of Salvation, to the *Correction* of Offenders, *Removing* of *Scandal,* and the *Deterring* of others? These are such clear and uncontroulable

troulable Evidences of the Neceſſity of Publick Eſtabliſhments, that we find them in all the *Churches* of the *Saints*, or Chriſtian World: and the Civil Government, agreeable to the Prophetick Character, is the profeſſed *Guardian*, and *Protector* of 'em.

Sect. VII. It now remains, *That we conſider the* Influences, *which the* Liberty *of the* Press *has upon an* Eſtabliſhment.

And certainly, where Men are under an unlimited Allowance to publiſh their Sentiments of things, it's the *Publick Eſtabliſhment*, that muſt ſuffer the ſharpeſt attack. It's this that bears the ſhew of *Authority* and *Dominion*, or ſtands between its Adverſaries, and ſome beloved Intereſts. It's the only Check to the Ambition, Avarice, Luxury, or Impurity of a *Licentious World*. When this is born down by *Calumny* and *Sophiſtry*, and brought into diſgrace, there's nothing left to obſtruct a general Licentiouſneſs. So that the greateſt Libertine may plead a Right, not only to erect his own Scheme, but to do whatever ſeemeth right in his own Eyes. And therefore, the common Torrent of Vice will

will not only bear down upon her; but those more active Furies, Envy, Malice, Prejudice, and Revenge, will unite to form an Indictment. In a word, an Establishment as such, is markt out as a Common *Enemy*, against whom every Tribe and Sect, of how different a Make and Complexion soever, are prepared to unite and arm: and when they may do it at so easie an Expence of Danger, or rather under the Banner of *Freedom* and *Liberty*, no wonder if they *shoot forth their Arrows, even bitter words;* and are content with nothing less, than reducing the whole Oeconomy to desolation and ruine.

SECT. VIII. GOD knows, we are not now left to view the force of the Argument, in empty *Theory* and *Notion*, since we may read it in Matter of *Fact*, and Observation. What Branch of our Establishment, of moment and importance, has the *Liberty* of the *Press* left free and untouched? Has not the *Divinity* of our SAVIOUR, and the whole Doctrine of the *Ever-blessed* TRINITY (as delivered in our Articles) been run down, and discarded, by a whole shoal of Pamphlets? Has not the whole Design of CHRIST's *Mission* been industriously overturned, and the Doctrine of His *Redemption* and *Satisfaction*, by the *Offering up* of *Himself,* been peremptorily rejected, as *groundless, absurd,* and *impossible* ? [See *Atheist turned Deist,* Sect. 42, 43, 47.] Has not Reason been asserted, to be the only Measure of Faith; so that whatever cannot be comprehended by it, is to be rejected from being an *Article of Faith*? [*Christianity not Mysterious*] Has not an Assent to this single Proposition, *Jesus of* Nazareth *is the Messiah,* been asserted to be the only explicite Article of Faith necessary to Salvation? [*The Reasonableness of Christianity,* p. 43, 49. 192.] Has not Revelation it self been disputed and rejected, as an incompetent Rule to Mankind! [*Oracles of Reason,* Let. 3. 14.]

Lastly, As to our Offices of Publick Worship: Has not the *Press* brought Scandal and Reproach, upon two of the Anniversary Solemnities of this Church, tho' enjoyned by Acts of *Parliament,* viz. The *Martyrdom of King* Charles *the First,* and the *Restauration of this Church and Mo-*

Monarchy, in the Return of King Charles *the Second?* For do we not find it exprefly vindicating the whole Scene of Violence, tranfacted in that Bloody War againſt the *King,* and ſtigmatizing the great Inſtruments of the *Reſtoration.* Nay more, we find the very *Author* applauding himſelf, as having a Point of Honour done him, by being choſen one of the *King's* Judges. [See *Milton's* Εἰκονοκλάςης, falſly pretended to be printed at *Amſterdam,* and *Ludlow's* Memoirs, *London, Vol.* 2d. *p.* 871.] Theſe are the bleſſed Products of the *Preſs,* laid open, and proſtituted to the Wit and Malice of deſigning Men; and yet they are but the ſmall Gleanings of that Maſs of Filth and Corruption, it has brought forth. And what can more directly tend to a total ſubverſion of an *Eſtabliſhment,* and more effectually prepare the World, to believe the Truth of their repeated Declamations; *viz.* That *Creeds and Syſtems, are only profitable Inventions,* or rather, That the whole *Oeconomy* of our *Eſtabliſhment* is but *Secular Policy,* and the Arts of *Prieſtcraft.* The *Preſs* has already publickly declared thus much; and that

Cold-

Coldneſs, or rather *Air* of *Contempt*, that too generally prevails againſt that of this *Church*, abundantly demonſtrates the pernicious Influences of it.

But now to improve the Argument: It's already concluded, That *Eccleſiaſtical Eſtabliſhments*, or *National Churches* are indiſpenſibly neceſſary; they reſt on the Authority of *Apoſtolick Inſtitution*, and are confirmed from the very Nature and Deſign of the *Chriſtian Religion*. It's concluded, That the *Chriſtian Magiſtrate* is by *Divine Appointment*, conſtituted a *Guardian* and *Protector* of *National Churches*, within his reſpective Dominions: It's a ſtanding Truſt committed to him by the Laws of *Natural*, as well as *Revealed Religion*: If therefore the *Liberty* of the *Preſs*, is highly deſtructive of the *Intereſts* of *Religion*, and particularly as 'tis cultivated in *National Churches:* If it appears not only in the Nature of the thing, but upon unqueſtionable Matter of *Fact*, the *Magiſtrate*, who by Divine Appointment is conſtituted a *Guardian* and *Protector* in the cauſe of *Religion*, is indiſpenſibly bound to remove the miſchief, by laying

a

a powerful Restraint on the *Press*. In a word, it is concluded, If a *National Establishment* is any way defective, or unsound in *Faith, Worship,* or *Discipline,* the *Magistrate* is to endeavour a Reform, in a *Regular* and *Canonical Method:* and this, I'm confident, was never declined by the *Established Church* of *England;* but if nothing of this Nature can, with any force of Argument or Reason, be charged upon *Her,* then the Magistrate, *ex officio,* is bound to *protect* and *defend* Her, in the Purity of Her *Faith* and *Worship,* and in Her just Rights and Immunities, *exclusive* of all other *Sects* and *Parties;* especially where the Publick Peace and Unity is attempted by 'em. If therefore the *Liberty* of the *Press* is apparently prejudicial to Her *Interests, Rights* and *Immunities,* or the Purity of her *Faith* and *Worship,* I cannot find how the Magistrate can fairly be supposed to discharge that Trust GOD has laid upon *Him,* without laying a publick Restraint upon it.

SECT. IX. But further: The Restraint of the *Press* is necessary, if we consider the
per-

pernicious Influences it casts upon *Religion* in *General*, as 'tis the direct *Inlet* to *Scepticism*, *Heresie*, and *Infidelity*. It's certain the Attempts of a Licentious *Press*, are almost infinite, and inconceivable. *Error*, as well as *Vice*, is extreamly prolifick, and even as numerous as the sand of the Sea; the most virulent Poison may be gilded over, and Varnish and Colour may be laid on the foulest Cause; and consequently the *Press* may be the Parent of the grossest Errors, under the Mask of *Innocence*, *Zeal*, or *Charity*. And truly, if *Experience*, and *Matter of Fact*, must decide the Controversie, we are convinced, that the Lewdest Notions that ever entered the Heart of Man, have been of late advanced from the *Press*. And moreover, the Mischiefs that are this way propagated, are much more fatal than any other.

First, Because 'tis the most *Effectual* way of *Communicating 'em*. A Transient Harangue or Discourse, tho' never so malignant, cannot be so entirely lodged in the *Memory*, as totally to infect the Judgement: and after this, it passes not much beyond the *Present Audience*. But the *Press*

Preſs is a ſtanding *Monument* and *Record*, that not only communicates the whole Poiſon, and leaves it to *reſt* upon the *Mind* or *Judgment*; but conveys it to *Poſterity*.

Again, as the Miſchief is more *ſucceſsfully propagated*; ſo 'tis more *difficultly removed*. The Men of Learning, Judgment, and Probity, may be engaged in Matters of too great Importance, to be at leiſure to obviate the *Miſchiefs* of every *Poiſonous Libel*; but if it happens to receive a juſt Confutation, it's odds it either reaches not the deluded *Reader*, or loſes its juſt Efficacy by not preſenting it ſelf before the *Infection* is rivetted, and the Defence of the Error become a *Point* of *Intereſt* or *Honour*.

But that which is more fatal than all this, is, an Unreſtrained *Preſs* gives a kind of *Imprimatur* to every thing that comes from it. As the Caſe ſtands, the Generality of Mankind are ſcarce able, or at leiſure to detect the falſe Colours of an *Artificial Harangue*; much leſs enter into the *Merits* of any particular *Controverſie*; and in theſe Caſes, where a right Judgment can-

cannot be made, every thing that appears in publick, muſt paſs for *Orthodox*, unleſs it has ſome publick *Note* of *Diſtinction* fixed upon it. So that the moſt *Heterodox Poſitions* in this Caſe reſt upon equal Authority with the moſt convincing Truths, till they have received a Cenſure from the *Government*, either in *Church* or *State*. And ſince *Paradoxes* are capable of receiving a *plauſible Dreſs*, and *Downright Contradictions* may be advanced, under a ſhew of *Argument*; what fatal Conſequences may not we juſtly dread, when *Religion* is the ſubject of both? The Injudicious and Illiterate *Reader* is expoſed to the Rack, and left to be divided and torn in pieces, between contrary Opinions; and either hangs ſo long between both, till he commences *Sceptick*, or *Infidel*, and *Believes Neither*; or at leaſt follows the Biaſs of *Luſt*, and *Corrupt Nature;* and is carried away with *Declamation* and *Harangue*, the *Uſual Artifices* of a *Bad Cauſe;* and conſequently is inevitably plunged into *Hereſie* and *Error*.

But further, the Miſchief riſes higher yet, for it's concluded, An Unreſtrained *Preſs*

Preß is often the moſt familiar with the *Eſtabliſhed Religion*, and never ſpares in bringing Diſgrace on any Branch, or part of it: It's the Publick Mark of *Envy* or *Malice*, and conſequently never wants the moſt Furious and Envenomed *Aſſailant*. But then, this is the direct *Method* to uſher in the moſt fatal Conſequences; for it will not only ſap the *Foundations* of an *Eſtabliſhment*, by bringing Her *Authority* into Contempt (it being the Moving Principle of all ſuch Attacks) but it ſtrikes at the *Reputation* of *Religion* in *General*, and makes way for reſolving the whole into *Sham*, and *Impoſture*. For when the *Government* ſuffers the *Preß* to attack a *Received Article* of the *Eſtabliſhed Religion*, without the leaſt *Cenſure*, or *Controul;* an indifferent Judge muſt conclude, that both cannot be true: And becauſe *Authority* does not proceed, to Aſſert and Vindicate its own *Eſtabliſhment*, or upon a fair Eſtimate, eſtabliſh and determine for the *Truth;* he'll conclude, there's no real Difference between *Truth* and *Falſhood*, and that *Religion it ſelf* is nothing but a Set of *Maxims*, calculated according to the ſeveral *Aſpects* and *Interests* of *Government*. This is so great a Truth, that I'm highly perswaded, those publick and repeated Attacks, made from the *Press* of late Years, upon the *Faith*, *Authority*, *Worship*, and *Discipline* of this *Church* (so many *Articles* of *Religion* having been so professedly questioned, and rejected) is the *Great Cause* of that *Scepticism* and *Infidelity*, or at least *Contempt* of *Religion*, which so visibly reigns in this *Nation*.

Give me leave to represent the Force of the present *Arguments*, in a single *Instance*. It's already concluded, that the *Press* has appeared in a Line of *Contradiction*, to two of our *Publick Offices* of *Worship*, the *Anniversaries* of that Glorious *Martyr King* Charles *the First*, and the *Restauration* of *King* Charles *the Second*. They are by *Royal Authority*, as well as *Statute-Law*, made part of our *Publick Service*. The whole Body of the *Clergy* are indispensibly bound to Celebrate them, and the whole *Legislative* Power, in a Solemn Manner, joyns in the *Celebration* of 'em; and yet we have Books publish'd in Contradiction to 'em; publish'd in the most open

open and audacious Manner. For the *Press* has not done its Duty, by sending 'em into the World, but they are publickly sold in the Shops, and exposed to sale from our *Publick Prints*, and *Term-Catalogues*. Now, what dismal Consequences can we imagine must attend such vile Practices? Our *Law-givers* piously declare, That *By the Murder of Our late Dread Sovereign*, *the* Protestant Religion *hath received the greatest Wound and Reproach, and the People of* England *the most insupportable Shame, that was possible for the Enemies of* GOD, *and the* King, *to bring upon us;* 12. *Car.* II. c. 30. But pardon me, if I pronounce the *Liberty of the Press*, to have advanced some Degrees beyond this: For the *Fact*, with its *Preliminaries*, is now not only levelled against the *Authority* of *Law*, and consequently that *Blasphemy*, and *Reproach* that is due to it, is renewed, and heightened; but a manifest *Blasphemy* and *Reproach* is entailed on the very Cause of *Religion:* Such Allowances as these, must cause the *Enemies* of GOD to *Blaspheme;* and tell us, that we either *Worship we know not what*, or that

our

our *Worship* is a Solemn piece of *Mockery*, or at least a piece of *Lip-Devotion;* or rather, that the whole of Religion is *Cheat* and *Imposture*. For if these things be reconcilable, there can be no *Truth* nor *Reality* in Religion; and this or that Profession, is no longer a piece of *Religion*, than it runs with the Tide and Bent of a Community.

But now when things discover such a fatal Tendency as this is, if there be any such thing as a *Guardian* of the *Church* of CHRIST, and if the *Magistrate* by *Divine Designation*, is invested with the *Character*, it must be an Indispensible Duty to exert with Vigour, and Resolution. The whole Case will turn upon a short Issue; if upon a Due and Regular *Examination*, these *Religious Offices* are *Materially Evil*, and *Unwarrantable;* let 'em be set aside, and abolished, that GOD may be no longer *trifled with* and *blasphemed;* nor His *Pastors* loaded with *Hatred* and *Contempt*, by being bound up to the Observance of things that are not Warrantable: But if notwithstanding the utmost Efforts of *Malice* and *Declamation*, they appear to be a *Pious* and a *Just Institution*, the *Magistrate*, if ever,

ever, muſt be obliged to endeavour a ſpeedy Redreſs; and ſince theſe Miſchiefs apparently derive from the *Liberty of the Preſs*, certainly the *Truſt* of a *Guardian* can never be diſcharged, without deſtroying the *Evil* in its *Cauſe:* and conſequently without laying a Powerful Reſtraint on it. When a Miſchief is thus dangerous, and deſtructive, it becomes the proper ſubject of a *Law*, and is to be ſuppreſſed with all the Enſigns of *Authority* and *Power*.

And now, *Sir*, I hope I have, in ſome meaſure, anſwered Your Demands, and diſcovered the *Neceſſity of Regulating the* Press; and that too with Regard to the *Eccleſiaſtical Eſtabliſhment* of *this Nation:* and therefore I'm inclined to perſwade my ſelf, the *Argument* will have its juſt Weight, and Influence on Your *Zeal* and *Affection*, for the Publick *Good*, as well as *Judgment*. But that nothing may intervene, to cauſe a Miſcarriage, I ſhall endeavour a ſhort return to the moſt *Conſiderable Objections*, that have been advanced againſt it.

Sect.

SECT. X. And, *first, It may be objected, That the Mischiefs of the* PRESS *may be effectually obviated, by* Particular Laws; *and that a* Restraint *of the* PRESS *from the Experience of former Times, has not prevented 'em.*

Now it must be confessed, That the *Law* produced in the last *Parliament*, may serve as a Bridle to the *Deist, Atheist,* and *Anti-Trinitarian;* but this can by no means obviate the Mischiefs of a *Licentious Press:* For there are other Truths, and Doctrines set forth in the *Christian Religion*, and this *Established Church;* which if publickly oppugned, must prove highly Injurious to the *Main Design* of the Christian Religion, as well as the *Peace* of the *Present Establishment*, such as the Doctrine of CHRIST's *Satisfaction*, by the *Sacrifice of Himself;* the Doctrine of *Grace,* or *Divine Assistance.* How these have of late suffered, the Publick has been too lately made a Witness, if not a Judge.

But certainly, the Mischiefs of the *Press* can never be fully obviated, unless by the *Restraint* of it; or at least, by such a *Law* as makes it highly *Penal*, to publish any thing

thing in Writing, that is level'd againſt any *Branch* of the *Eſtabliſhed Religion*; for ſince *National Eſtabliſhments* appear to be abſolutely Neceſſary for the Carrying on the Ends and Deſigns of the *Goſpel*, that which is amiſs is to be regularly corrected; and after this is done, nothing is to be ſuffered, that any-wiſe invades the *Peace* of ſuch an *Eſtabliſhment*.

But after all, *Penal Laws* of this Nature, are not ſo apt Inſtruments to prevent the Miſchiefs that uſually ſpring from the *Preſs*, as an abſolute *Reſtraint* of it, when the Authority of a *Licenſe* or *Imprimatur* is wanting. Such a *Reſtraint* deſtroys the Miſchiefs in its *Seeds* and *Principles*; it ſtops the Contagion in the very *Spring* or *Fountain*: whereas ſuch *Laws* take place at a Diſtance, it may be when the Infection is propagated to a conſiderable Degree.

There is a ſolemn Proceſs, and a great many Formalities, and Steps to be made, which may ſerve as ſo many Advantages, or Chances, to eſcape the *Force* of the *Law*. The *Author* is not only to be diſcovered, but an *Information* given in, and received too, according to the *Genius* and *Temper* of the *Magistrate;* and consequently the *Undertaker* must have Courage enough to bear the Title of *Informer;* an Office, which as the World goes, neither the *Justice* nor *Merits* of the Cause can secure from *Ignominy* and *Contempt*. Again; there must be a Prosecution by course of *Law*, and the Case examined, and tried whether it falls within the Penalty of the *Law;* and all this, perhaps, without the least Recompence to the *Prosecutor*, for *Expences* or *Attendance*. In a word, a Verbal Recantation, after the Labour and Difficulties of Conviction, may render the Author *Rectum in Curia:* and after this, he may under Disguise go afresh to work, at the small hazard of the least of Punishments. I wish some Provisions of this Nature had not been wanting in the late *Act against Profaneness and Immorality*, whereby a Pious Design may become Insignificant and Useless. For upon this bottom, while the *Press* is open, I'm afraid the Enemies of our Establishment will publish their Notions, with the Satisfaction of secret Smiles and Triumphs.

But

But now if the *Preſs* were ſhut, till an *Imprimatur* is obtained, the mere want of one is a *Competent Evidence* for Conviction; and tho' ſome may be ſo daring to expoſe their *Notions*, at the hazard of their *Safety*, yet ſuch a Reſtraint of the *Preſs* gives this conſiderable Advantage, That whatever comes forth without Authority, carries its own *Mark* in the *Title-page;* and conſequently gives an Alarm to the incautious READER, of *Infection* and *Miſchief*.

SECT. XI. But *Secondly, it is objected, That ſuch a Reſtraint of the* PRESS *is a giving up the Conſciences, and Judgments of Mankind to a Party, and a condemning them to an Implicit Faith, and is a direct Method to involve the World in Ignorance and Error.*

As for the *Firſt part* of the *Objection;* If an *Orthodox National Church* is the *Party* intended, I may ſafely affirm, That as it is the Duty of every Perſon within her Communion, to conform to her *Faith, Worſhip* and *Government;* ſo I hope it already appears, that it's a ſtanding Duty in the *Magistrate*, as well as *Church Governours*, not only to enforce all *Gospel* Means to bring every Soul into the Pale of it; but to *Maintain* and *Cultivate* the Purity of its *Faith* and *Worship*, against all the Attempts of its Enemies. If any thing is unsound and deficient, GOD has invested a Power of using such proper Means in the Governours of his Church, and the *Believing Magistrate*, as under his Divine Protection, will secure a True and Orthodox Religion; but if nothing of this Nature can be truly charged upon Her, when Endeavours have been made in this kind, tho' there may be no foundation, by Violence and Force, to compel Men to be of *one Mind*, and *one Heart;* yet the Magistrate is of *Right*, as well as *Duty*, bound not to suffer her *Peace* to be *Disturbed*, or her *Faith* and *Worship shaken* by *Publick Harangues*, and *Professed Declamations:* This is no Persecution, but a Necessary Provision, whereby the Designs of an important Trust committed to the Magistrate, are fulfilled and answered, I mean that of a *Guardian;* and since it is so, I cannot imagine why any Government should

[53]

should be flack in the Exercise of a *Just Power*; especially since all sides are sensible how much *Unanimity*, in Matters of Religion, contributes to the *Publick Weal* of a Nation. And truly, if to this Just Law, another as *Equitable* were established, *That Persons who will not content 'emselves with the Communion of the Established Religion, should thereby be uncapable of any Places of Trust or Office, either in Church or State;* as we find it in Neighbour Countries, I question not but it would have produced a greater *Unanimity* in Matters of Religion, than the most hopeful Projects of *Comprehension*. As the Case now stands, the Tolerated Party is envigorated with the Hopes of one Day reducing every thing to their own Model; but certainly had an *Incapaciting Clause* been fixed to the last *Act of Grace*, I mean that of *Toleration*, it would not only have proved an invincible Bulwark to our Pure and *Apostolick Establishment*, but the most Healing Principle of Unity that could have been contrived, or thought of.

SECT.

SECT. XII. But to return: As to the Charge of *Implicit Faith*, it must be confessed, That the Depriving Mankind of any of those Means, or Instruments which GOD has appointed for the Discovery of His *Revealed Will*, is a direct Invasion of the *Privileges* of a *Christian*, and a considerable step towards the Introduction of an *Implicit Faith*. But I presume it cannot be pretended, that an *Unlimited Power* of *Printing* is one of those *Means* which GOD has appointed for the Discovery of the True Religion. If so, GOD seems to have been very much wanting to his own Designs, in not communicating the Art by some *Apostle* or *Prophet*, long before it obtained in the Christian World. But it's well known, the True Religion rests upon other Foundations; it was *Established* in *Purity* and *Perfection*, long before this useful Art was formed, or thought of; and I question not, will long continue so, unless the *Privilege* of *Printing* the *lewdest* and most *Heretical Notions*, subvert its Foundations.

As for this *National Establishment*, I challenge her most avowed Enemies to pro-

produce one single Instance, wherein she denies her Members the use of any *Divine* or *Apostolick Means*, that are Instituted for the Discovery of the True Religion. Our Church imposes no Article of Faith upon pure Church-authorities; she recommends every thing to the Mind and Conscience upon rational Motives, and Convictions: She is careful to publish useful Discourses, in Matters of Faith and Practice; and, in a word, every thing *that is profitable for Doctrine, for Reproof, for Correction, for Instruction in Righteousness, that the Man of* God *may be perfect, throughly furnished unto all good Works.* She does not only allow, but exhort her People, *To examine themselves whether they are in the Faith:* She denies 'em no Means of Information, she does not only lay open the Well of Life, or Fountain of Living Waters, the *Holy Scriptures,* but recommends 'em to their Search and Enquiry, even to the Trying *of the Spirits* by them: She allows 'em to propose their Doubts and Scruples to their *Spiritual Pastors,* and administers Counsel and Advice upon the force of *Reason* and *Scripture:*

pture. In a word, as she conceals nothing of the *whole Counsel of* God, so she admits all their Proposals, by way of *Enquiry* and *Information:* So that there is nothing wanting of those Means God has instituted to enable every Man *To give a reason of the Hope that is in him*.

Where then is that *Nursery* of *Implicit Faith* and *Ignorance?* If Mens Judgments by all these Methods cannot, or will not be set right and informed, shall they challenge a Right to publish Dogmatically, what they pretend to retain on no other Authority, than that of a weak Conscience, to bear down *a rightful Establishment?* Are all the *Means* of *Information* useless, and to be despised, if this is not suffered? Must they from *Examiners* and *Enquirers*, immediately commence *Doctors* and *Dictators;* and deliver their Sentiments with equal Authority to that of the *Established Religion?* Where is that *Spiritual Tyranny*, or *Blind Obedience*, when they may propose their *Arguments*, *Doubts*, and *Scruples* to *Private Pastors*, or a *Publick Convocation;* when they may depute *Proxies*, and be admitted to *Conferences*, and

and *Publick Debates*, without *Passes* of *Safety*, without the Dread of an *Inquisition*, or of a *Writ de Hæretico comburendo*? These are Privileges that may be obtained for asking; and they are the most apposite Methods for the distinguishing Truth from Falshood: They are such as GOD has appointed, and consequently such as GOD may be presumed to give a Blessing to. When therefore an Establishment has done all this, shall the Magistrate that is constituted a *Guardian*, and *Trustee* in the *Church* of CHRIST, suffer the Consciences of Men to be distracted, and the *Publick Peace* of the *Church* invaded, by the bold Cavils and Harangues of every *Unreasonable Gainsayer*?

SECT. XIII. *Thirdly*, 'Tis objected, *That every one, not only of* Natural Right, *but in point of* Duty, *particularly that of* Charity, *may and ought to publish whatever appears to be* Truth, *for the Information and Direction of others; and consequently the Restraint of the* Press, *that abridges this Right, must be unlawful, and unjust.*

But, *First*, it's an indisputable Truth, That the *Natural Rights* and *Duties* of *Private Persons*, are perpetually consonant to the *Rights* and *Interests* of *Publick Societies*; and the Exercise of the former, is for the most part to be regulated, and determined by the latter. Again, Whatever the Rights and Interests of Private Persons may be, the Magistrate is absolutely entrusted with the Preservation of the Publick Peace; and consequently may rightfully suppress every thing that is level'd against any Branch of the *Publick Establishment;* since such Attempts unsettle the Minds of a People, and engender intemperate Heats and Animosities, and consequently carry a direct Tendency to Disorder and Confusion.

All Governments give a latitude for *private Opinions* and *Sentiments;* and therefore do not usually extend their *Tests* or *Subscriptions*, beyond Places of *Trust* or *Publick Employments:* whereas 'tis their Care and Prudence to keep a watchful Eye upon *New Notions* obtruded on the Publick. Whilst an Opinion rests in the *Breasts* of private Persons, the *Publick Peace* is not ex-

exposed; but when 'tis pressed upon Mankind in *Publick Harangues*, and transmitted from the *Press* too; it gives Umbrage to the Peace and Weal of the Community, and consequently calls for the Care and Vigilance of the Magistrate. In Cases of this Nature, the first Christian Emperors appear'd as *Guardians* in the Church of CHRIST, and vigorously exerted their Power and Authority, to maintain its publick Peace and Unity.

SECT. XIV. *As for the Duty of Communicating our Opinions to others, with a Design of Information, it is indisputably to be regulated by two* Considerations.

First, The *Importance* of the *Opinion*, and *Secondly*, The *Certainty* and *Evidence* of it.

First, If the Opinion be such as does not affect any considerable Interest of Mankind, or correct or remove any dangerous Error, but rather serves to entertain our *Speculation* and *Curiosity*, than regulate our *Conscience* or *Practice*; there can be no Obligation to disturb the World by opposing *Established Doctrines* or *Notions*, when after all they may carry in them greater Marks or Evidences of Truth, than a private Judgment can reasonably pretend to.

Secondly, Unless our Opinions are supported by the clearest Convictions of *Reason*, or *Authority* of *Scripture*, (as all matters of Importance undoubtedly are) there can be no just Plea for *Duty*, to engage the rest of the World to become *Disciples* or *Followers*. And indeed it seems highly unreasonable, that private Persons should amuse the Minds of others by obtruding *New Notions*, when it may be they rest upon bare *Probabilities*, or no higher Evidences than those that have been *peaceably* received from *Publick Authority* in *Church* and *State*. If the Projections and Opinions of Men were governed by these Maxims, I'm perswaded the *Restraint* of the *Press* (when it is thereby only committed to the Inspection of *Publick Authority*) would seldom be interpreted a Breach of any *Natural Rights* or *Duties*.

Sect. XV. There now only remains an Objection no way worthy to be animadverted on, on, except for its *Popularity* and *Modern Fashionableness:* 'Tis this, *That the Restraint of the* PRESS, *is an Invasion of the Liberty and Property of an* Englishman.

But I'm perswaded before the Objection can justly take place, the *Privileges* of the *Press* should be discovered to be an *Article* of *Magna Charta*, tho' it were some Centuries before *Printing* had its Beginning: But in a word, if the Power of Legislation is to be crampt, and fettered in the Case before us, I cannot see but that every Authoritative Regulation of the Actions of an *English* Subject, might be disputed as a Breach of the *Liberty* and *Property* of an *Englishman*, and consequently no Law could be established, without first obtaining the Unanimous Consent of the People.

SECT. XVI. And now, *Sir*, I have in some measure dispatched what I proposed, and You seem to have demanded; and tho' I have not expresly replied to Your Enquiries in the very Terms, or order they were proposed; yet I have the Vanity to presume, That I have not only made returns to the Arguments contained in them; but

but dispel'd that Cloud of Objections that of late has been raised to obstruct the Restraint of the *Press*. If therefore what has been already offered has the good Fortune to carry the Balance, against Your former Sentiments, be pleased to suffer a short Address on my part, in the case before us, as a hearty Advocate for the Maintainance and Welfare of the *Government* in *Church* and *State*.

Sir, We have been hitherto engaged in the Cause of Religion, and the Methods of its Preservation and Support. And the late passionate Address of the last *Parliament*, and His *Majesty's* most Gracious Answer to it, seems to Authorize the Pursuit of the Argument. That *Venerable Body* wisely applied Themselves to their *Sovereign,* to consult His *Pleasure,* as well as excite His *Zeal* and *Piety*: and He was pleased to signifie His concurrence, and remit the Managery of the Affair to His *House of Commons,* as to the proper *Instruments* to prepare Matters for the Formation of a just Law. It's true, that *Honourable House* formed a Bill upon the present Argument; but the Miscarriages of it, it, where-ever juftly to be fixed, cannot conclude againft the Reafonablenefs or Neceffity of it. I'm confident the Eyes and Heart, the Hopes and Expectations of every *Englifhman*, that is acted with a true Concern for the True Religion, are fixed on the enfuing Seffion ; and pardon me, if I flatter My-felf, That the Arguments already fuggefted, demonftrate the abfolute Neceffity of Reftraining the *Prefs*, as an effectual Expedient to preferve the Interefts of it.

The Liberty of Printing without Licenfe or Infpection, has fufficiently difcharged its poifonous Influences againft the *Interefts* of the *Eftablifhed Religion ;* and a fmall tract of Time in the fame Allowance, would demonftrate its Force and Efficacy againft the Interefts of the *Civil Polity*, as eftablifhed in a *Monarchy*. I wifh fome late Effays had not afferted the Truth of the Obfervation: witnefs thofe grofs Infinuations the *Prefs* has prefented us with, for the preference of a *Republick* to that of *Monarchy*: [See *Ludlow's Memoirs*] Witnefs thofe bafe and unwarrantable Characters vented in a late Paper, where-

wherein the present Reign seems to be blacken'd by the Help of a *Prophetick Spirit*, and making it an Accessary to what may come hereafter; where every Estate of the Realm, and every Order of Men in Authority and Places of Trust, are described like Ruffians and Paltroons, rather than Persons of Dignity and Honour. What can be the Scope of such unmannerly Declamation, but to bring the *English* Constitution into Disgrace, and prepare the Minds of the People for *Anarchy* and Confusion. [See *The short History of Standing Armies in England*.]

But to return: You, *Sir*, and Your *Honourable Brethren*, are concerned as Trustees and Guardians in part for *Religion;* and since the necessity of a National Establishment is fully demonstrated, all disinterested Persons must conclude, That Your special Care and Inspection should be engaged to advance that of this Nation, of which You profess Your selves *Members*, and from whose *Communion*, by Civil Appointment, You receive Qualifications for *Places* of *Trust*, or *Publick Employ*. A Temporary Interest may engage a great many

many Men, to declare 'emselves *Members* of Her Communion; but it's certain the true Test of *Membership* is to use all imaginable Endeavours to maintain her *Rights*, and support her *Constitution;* whenever she's publickly attack'd in any Branch of it.

To have the *Press* regulated by the received Doctrines of a *National Establishment*, is to be esteemed one of her *undoubted Rights* and *Immunities;* and therefore when Invasions of this Nature are daily made, she may justly expect the interposal of *Authority:* But if she could not challenge thus much of Right, yet since the *Dissenting Sectaries* have received very ample *Acts* of *Grace*, under the *present Government;* the *Established Religion*, one would think, may reasonably expect her tail in this kind, and command the *Press* in matters of Religion, as the *First Act* of *Grace;* especially since 'tis no more but what *Former Reigns*, by an indisputable Authority, afforded her.

But to draw towards a Conclusion: Give me leave to tell You, *Sir*, If the *Restraint* of the *Press* cannot be obtained by way of Right,

Right, nor Grace and Favour: I queſtion not but the fatal influences it has upon *Morality* and *Religion,* is Motive ſufficient to accompliſh it. I ſhall not reſume the Argument I have already enlarged on; but certainly it ſeems to be a fruitleſs Attempt to ſuppreſs *Immorality* and *Profaneneſs,* and eſtabliſh a Sence of *Religion,* and *Principle* of *Piety,* whilſt a latitude is permitted in the moſt publick manner, to diſpute the moſt *Sacred Points* of *Religion,* to decry *National Eſtabliſhments,* arraign the whole Order of the *Miniſters* of *Religion,* and the Solemnities of *Publick Worſhip.* It's impoſſible the generality of Mankind under theſe Inſtructions, can entertain any ſerious Thoughts concerning *Religion,* but are rather prepared to contemn and vilifie the *Bleſſed* AUTHOR of it, and the whole *Contrivance:* and therefore if *Morality* and ſtrict *Vertue* is purſued on theſe terms, it's more to be aſcribed to the happy *Genius* of Mankind, than any Principle of Religion. In a word then, If the Honourable Aſſembly of *Commons* is in earneſt for *Reformation* (as I queſtion not but they are) what has already been offered,
ſeems

seems to bespeak the *Regulation* of the *Press* to be the most likely *Introduction* to it.

And now, *Sir*, I have delivered my Sentiments with as much Sincerity as Freedom. All that remains, is, If they happen to make You a *Proselyte*, I hope You'll employ Your hearty Endeavours, in the Post You're fixt, to make the Argument the subject of a Law; and the greatest Testimony of this will be, that Care be taken, not only that a Law be formed, which will effectually answer the Designs of it; but that the Forming of it be done with that Prudence and Caution, as not to give a handle to crush it in its first Production. When this is accomplished, it will lay perpetual Obligations of Gratitude and Respect towards the Instruments of it, on all those in whom the Interest of this Government apparently consists; *The True Members of the Established* CHURCH *of* ENGLAND.

FINIS.

ERRATA.

Pag. 1. *lin.* 1. *read* solicite. *p.* 24. *l.* 20. *read* Eternal. *p.* 49. *l.* 4. *dele* absolutely. *p.* 65. *l.* 20. *read* Tale.